YOUTH WHO ARE GIFTED

Integrating Talents and Intelligence

HELPING YOUTH WITH MENTAL, PHYSICAL, AND SOCIAL CHALLENGES

Title List

YOUTH WHO ARE GIFTED

Integrating Talents and Intelligence

by Sheila Nelson and Phyllis Livingston

Mason Crest Publishers
Philadelphia

Mason Crest Publishers Inc.
370 Reed Road
Broomall, Pennsylvania 19008
(866) MCP-BOOK (toll free)
www.masoncrest.com

First printing

1 2 3 4 5 6 7 8 9 10

ISBN 978-1-4222-0133-6 (series)

Library of Congress Cataloging-in-Publication Data

Nelson, Sheila.
   Youth who are gifted : integrating talents and intelligence / by Sheila Nelson and Phyllis Livingston.
      p. cm. — Includes bibliographical references and index.
   ISBN-13: 978-1-4222-0135-0 (alk. paper)
   1. Gifted teenagers. 2. Adolescent psychology. I. Livingston, Phyllis, 1957– II. Title.
BF724.3.G53N45 2008
305.9'089—dc22
2007010779

Interior pages produced by
Harding House Publishing Service, Inc.
www.hardinghousepages.com
Interior design by MK Bassett-Harvey.
Cover design by MK Bassett-Harvey.
Cover Illustration by Keith Rosko.
Printed in the Hashemite Kingdom of Jordan.

The creators of this book have made every effort to provide accurate information, but it should not be used as a substitute for the help and services of trained professionals.

Contents

Introduction

We are all people first, before anything else. Our shared humanity is more important than the impressions we give to each other by how we look, how we learn, or how we act. Each of us is worthy simply because we are all part of the human race. Though we are all different in many ways, we can celebrate our differences as well as our similarities.

In this book series, you will read about many young people with various special needs that impact their lives in different ways. The disabilities are not *who* the people are, but the disabilities are an important characteristic of each person. When we recognize that we all have differing needs, we can grow toward greater awareness and tolerance of each other. Just as important, we can learn to accept our differences.

Not all young people with a disability are the same as the persons in the stories. But you will learn from these stories how a special need impacts a young person, as well as his or her family and friends. The story will help you understand differences better and appreciate how differences make us all stronger and better.

—*Cindy Croft, M.A.Ed.*

Did you know that as many as 8 percent of teens experience anxiety or depression, and as many as 70 to 90 percent will use substances such as alcohol or illicit drugs at some time? Other young people are living with life-threatening diseases including HIV infection and cancer, as well as chronic psychiatric conditions such as bipolar disease and schizophrenia. Still other teens have the challenge of being "different" from peers because they are intellectually gifted, are from another culture, or have trouble controlling their behavior or socializing with others. All youth with challenges experience additional stresses compared to their typical peers. The good news is that there are many resources and supports available to help these young people, as well as their friends and families.

The stories contained in each book of this series also contain factual information that will enhance your own understanding of the particular condition being presented. If you or someone you know is struggling with a similar condition or experience, this series can give you important information about where and how you can get help. After reading these stories, we hope that you will be more open to the differences you encounter in your peers and more willing to get to know others who are "different."

—*Carolyn Bridgemohan, M.D.*

Chapter 1

Unacceptable Behavior

I knew it was going to be a bad day when I fell asleep in history class. Mr. Tepper was droning on and on about some battle that happened in some year, and I just couldn't listen to it. Who cared, really? I mean, you'd think a battle should be interesting, but no, not after Mr. Tepper got a hold of it. He didn't tell us about the men who were terrified to fight but went anyway, or about the women who were left at home taking care of the babies and not knowing whether their husbands would ever come home, or whether the enemy would suddenly descend on them and burn their houses to the ground. He didn't tell us about the young boys (and girls) who disguised themselves and snuck into the army because they wanted to do something to help their country. If he'd said any of that I would have listened to him, because, really, I know history can be interesting as long as you're reading stories about it instead of sitting in history class listening to Mr. Tepper say, "And in 18-whatever, the situation became tenser until finally the whoever declared war on the other guys. The battle of whatever took place somewhere and lasted for some amount of days." Of course, he filled in details instead of saying whatever, whoever, or somewhere, but, as I said, I wasn't listening.

"Ann!" said a voice somewhere over my head. For a minute, I didn't move, but slowly I realized that my head was resting on my arm on my desk and Mr. Tepper was standing over me. I looked up and the whole class was staring at me. Most of them were laughing. And worst of all, Rob Spanogle, the cutest guy in class, was staring and laughing right along with them. Oh, how embarrassing. I thought I was going to die.

"Late night last night, Ann?" Mr. Tepper asked sarcastically.

"Sorry," I said. And then I tried to focus on my notebook instead of looking at him. I didn't answer his question because, first of all, I assumed it was rhetorical and, second of all, I really was up late the night before. I'd been on the computer writing code for this online game I was helping to design, and I think it was after three when I finally went to bed.

Mr. Tepper stood there for a long time, and I could feel his eyes boring into the back of my head. I kept pretending to reread my notes (there weren't a lot of them). Finally, Mr. Tepper said, "This is unacceptable behavior, Ann. I expect you to pay attention in my class."

I said, "Yes, Mr. Tepper," without looking up, and after a few more seconds he walked back to the front of the room and started talking about the boring battle again. To keep myself awake for the rest of the class, and to look like I was taking notes, I wrote a poem about Rob Spanogle.

When the bell rang for lunch, I got out of there as fast as I could. I think Mr. Tepper was trying to get my attention, but I didn't look at him. I didn't feel like listening to any more about my "unacceptable behavior." Besides, I was hungry.

After school, I went to the library. I love the library. It's very small—like everything in Mill Creek—and I've read most of the interesting books, but it has a few big, comfortable armchairs, and I can curl up and read or write or even fall asleep without being yelled at. I didn't want to go home, partly because I was pretty sure my brother Daniel would have heard about history class and he would probably tell Mom.

Daniel is sixteen—two years older than me—and, even though he has some good points, he can be very annoying. For one thing, he's perfect. He's tall and good-looking and popular. He gets straight A's and all the teachers love him. He plays soccer and basketball and dates cheerleaders. I, on the other hand, am not good-looking, not popular, not athletic, and I fall asleep in history class.

I was lying across one of the chairs, flipping through a magazine, when Rob Spanogle and his friends Jason White and Hunter Keyes walked up.

"Hey," Rob said to his friends, "it's the bookworm. So *Ann*"—somehow he made my name sound like an insult— "I always thought Tepper's class was boring, but aren't you supposed to be some kind of a brain who likes that stupid stuff? Is it true you fell asleep because you were studying all night?"

I blushed, which annoyed me because now they were going to think it was true. All of a sudden, Rob was not as cute as he had been. "No," I said. "The truth is, I was sleepy because I stole my dad's motorcycle last night and drove into the city where I hung out with my cousin and her gangbanger friends until dawn. But I could hardly tell Tepper that, could I?"

Rob stared at me like I'd just grown a third eye in my forehead. I don't know why I said that. Of course, my dad doesn't even have a motorcycle, and my only cousins are eight-year-old twin boys who live two thousand miles away. I just get really annoyed with being called a brain. Usually I don't say much and people are always calling me quiet— which I also hate. But, sometimes, I open my mouth and something like that pops out. It's strange. I regretted it almost immediately, because I could imagine the kind of stories that would be going around in school tomorrow, but I did like that stunned look on Rob's face.

"Oh," said Rob, and I could tell he couldn't think of anything to say to that. Jason looked about as startled as Rob, but Hunter was laughing a little bit, like he appreciated my humor. Hunter was new this year, and he'd taken up with Rob and his group almost immediately. I didn't really know anything about him, but I looked at him with new interest.

"Let's go shoot some hoops," Rob said to his friends, and they left, Hunter smiling at me.

As soon as they were gone, I opened my notebook and ripped out the page that had the poem I'd written about Rob. Then I ripped the poem into very tiny pieces, carried them into the bathroom, and flushed them down the toilet.

I made it home right before supper. Mom was setting the table when I came in. "Where have you been?" she asked. "Wash your hands and finish this while I take the chicken out of the oven." She dumped the silverware onto the table and flitted over to the other side of the kitchen.

My mother is a very intense person. She's brilliant, but also very changeable. For example, she used to be kind of a modern hippy, back when she was in college. She wore only natural fibers and didn't eat meat and went to protests. She met Dad in a biology class and dazzled him with her enthusiastic personality. Then she sucked him into the protest scene and married him after she got pregnant with Daniel. After graduation, though, when Dad got a job managing one of his uncle's furniture stores, she gave up the hippy thing and threw herself into being the perfect stay-at-home mom. The real secret in our family is that Ann isn't really my name, and Daniel isn't really my brother's name. Those are our middle names, but our first names are hippy names. Daniel's first name is Sequoia, and mine is Morning-Glory. Mom stopped using those names as soon as we drove away from San Francisco in the moving truck, leaving them behind with her ankle-length cotton skirts. I didn't care at the time, since I was only six months old, but it had apparently been very confusing for poor Daniel who was over two.

"I heard you fell asleep in class," Daniel said as we ate, and I kicked him under the table. I had really been hoping he hadn't heard.

"Not really," I said, glaring at him. "I just closed my eyes for a minute to think, and Mr. Tepper *thought* I was asleep."

"That's not what I heard," he said. "I heard Mr. Tepper stood there calling your name for two minutes and you didn't wake up. And you were snoring," he added.

"I was *not* snoring!" I exclaimed, horrified, and thought, oh, please let me not have been snoring.

"You fell asleep in class?" Dad asked, putting down his fork.

"Mr. Tepper is your history teacher, isn't he? Oh, Ann, you're too smart to be messing with your future like this," Mom said.

"I dozed off for a minute in *one* class. That's hardly messing with my future." But of course, my parents know that I'm not doing very well in history. And that's because Mr. Tepper doesn't talk about anything interesting. I'm also not doing very well in math, because I don't care, or in biology, because I keep refusing to do any of the dissections—not exactly on moral grounds but because they're gross—and I am consequently failing the labs. My grades are an interesting mix of B's and D's with a few A's thrown in.

"You could do so much with your life," Dad said, "but you have to choose to shape up and do the work."

"But I'm not going to do anything that has to do what Mr. Tepper talks about," I said, which of course was the wrong thing to say.

"That is the wrong attitude, young lady," Dad said.

"We had your IQ tested once," Mom said, like I was hoping she wouldn't. "Yours and Daniel's. You're both smart enough to be called geniuses, and yours was even a few points higher than Daniel's. But no one would know it to watch you. You're going to waste your life if you keep going like this. Why can't you try to be more like your brother?"

That was the question I hated more than anything.

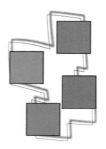

What Does It Mean to Be Gifted?

According to Merriam-Webster's dictionary, to be gifted means to have "great natural ability." In one sense of the word, we are all gifted: one person may have a natural ability for sports, another for music, and another for math, while still other individuals may have a natural ability for making friends, making people laugh, or working with animals. These sorts of gifts come in many shapes and sizes, and it's important to recognize and appreciate their reality, both in ourselves and in others. We're not all good at the same things—but we all have something special and unique to offer the world.

Each one of us has been given unique gifts; our job is to discover them and share them with the world.

That's why some people are uncomfortable using the word "gifted" for just one type of gift—intellectual intelligence and creativity—because it implies a value judgment; it seems to indicate that people who are smart and creative are somehow different and better than other people. Sometimes others resent people like this. Sometimes people who are "gifted" in this sense of the word may feel embarrassed or uncomfortable with the label—or on the flip side of the coin, they may feel conceited and arrogant. In either case, they're focusing on what makes them different, rather than on all the ways that human beings are all alike, whether or not they score well on intelligence tests. Ultimately, what makes us alike

No matter what our various gifts may be, when we share them with each other we make the human community stronger.

as human beings is more important than what makes us different.

Many of the world's great leaders and inventors, however—people like Einstein and Leonardo da Vinci, Madame Curie, and Mother Teresa—were "gifted": they had something special to offer, and because they shared their gifts with those around them, they helped change the world. In the twentieth century, educators and governments recognized that these "special" people are important to our world; as a result, schools and governments worked to create educational programs that would nurture and develop future leaders.

Who Do Schools Label as Gifted?

In 1971, Sidney P. Marland Jr., the former U.S. Commissioner of Education, stated in report to Congress:

> Gifted and talented children are those identified by professionally qualified persons who by virtue of outstanding abilities are capable of high performance. These are children who require differentiated educational programs and/or services beyond those normally provided by the regular school program in order to realize their contribution to self and society.

In many cases, schools and the public in general equate the words "gifted" and "highly intelligent." From this perspective, a student's IQ test will indicate whether she is gifted. The commonly used ranges of giftedness are:

moderately gifted are students who have an IQ between 130 and 145 (an "average" IQ is 100)

highly gifted are students with IQs between 145 and 160

extremely gifted are students with IQs between 160 and 180

profoundly gifted are students with an IQ over 180

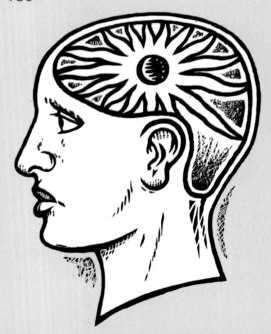

Scientists and educators have tried to put numbers to human intelligence. Ultimately, however, the human brain's abilities are difficult to test and measure.

What Is IQ?

IQ stands for "intelligence quotient," a number derived from special **standardized** tests scientifically designed to measure a person's ability to conduct a number of tasks to which most people raised in that society will be exposed. These tests, which are administered by trained professionals, measure a person's ability to absorb and repeat mechanical and intellectual tasks. The quotient originally referred to the ratio between a person's "mental age" (as determined by the test) divided by his actual chronological age, and then multiplied by one hundred.

In other words, if a child was five years old but achieved a score of seven years on an IQ test, her IQ would be determined with this equation:

$$7 \div 5 = 1.4 \times 100 = 140$$

Using this equation had problems, however, since as a person grew older, it would look as though his IQ grew lower (which isn't normally the case). Today, IQ is determined by comparing a person's score to a table that indicates percentiles for that person's age.

Nowadays, most people equate the term "IQ" with intelligence, but before the twentieth century, the concept of IQ did not exist. No one had ever considered that human ability was something that could be measured. As the scientific revolution moved through **Western** culture, however, people became obsessed with measuring most everything, from the circumference of the Earth . . . to human intelligence. As French philosopher René Descartes said in the seventeenth century, "If something exists, it exists in some amount. If it exists in some amount, then it is capable of being measured."

Intelligence testing began in France in 1904, when the French government commissioned psychologist Alfred Binet to find a method to differentiate between children who were intellectually normal and those who were inferior; those who were "inferior" would be put into special schools, where they would receive more individual attention while avoiding the disruption they caused in the education of intellectually "normal" children.

This led to the development of the Binet Scale (also known as the Simon-Binet Scale in recognition of Theophile Simon's assistance in its development). The test had children do tasks such as follow commands, copy patterns, name objects, and put things in order or arrange them properly. Binet gave the test to Paris schoolchildren and created a standard based on his data.

Binet's test was a revolutionary approach to determining intellectual ability. However, Binet himself cautioned against misusing the scale or misunderstanding its implications. The scale was designed with a single purpose in mind, Binet insisted: to serve only as a guide for identifying students who could benefit from extra help in school. His assumption was that a lower IQ indicated the need for more teaching, not an inability to learn. According to Binet, the test was not intended to be used as "a general device for ranking all pupils according to mental worth." Binet also noted that "the scale, properly

Alfred Binet might be considered the first school psychologist; he was the father of the intelligence test that is administered today by school psychologists who are assessing the learning needs of students.

Stanford University in California was the birthplace of the American version of Binet's intelligence test, the Stanford-Binet.

speaking, does not permit the measure of intelligence, because intellectual qualities . . . cannot be measured as linear surfaces are measured." Binet feared that IQ measurement could be used to condemn a child to a permanent "condition of stupidity," which would negatively affect her education and livelihood.

Binet's scale had a profound impact on U.S. schools—but American educators and psychologists failed to heed Binet's warning concerning its limitations. Soon, intelligence testing became a vital part of how educators (and the rest of the world) looked at individuals.

H. H. Goddard, director of research at Vineland Training School in New Jersey, decided that the Binet test would be a wonderful way to screen students for his school, so he translated Binet's work into English and advocated a more general application of the Simon-Binet Scale. Goddard used the scale to sort people into several categories:

- geniuses (people who had an IQ above 140)
- normal (people with IQs between 70 and 130)
- morons (people with IQs between 50 and 70, with a mental age of more than seven years but less than that of a "normal" person's)
- imbeciles (people with IQs between 25 and 50, who could only develop to a mental age of three to seven years)
- idiots (people with IQs between 0 and 25, who could not progress past the mental age of a three-year-old)

Unlike Binet, Goddard believed intelligence was a fixed and inborn quality that could be measured.

Other American educators agreed, and Stanford University commissioned the creation of a revised version of Binet's test; the final product, published in 1916 as the *Stanford Revision of the Binet-Simon Scale of Intelligence* (also known as the *Stanford-Binet*), became the standard intelligence test in the United States for the next several decades.

Americans became convinced that intelligence tests were accurate, scientific, and valuable tools that would make schools more efficient. Few educators realized, however, that many of the Americans who had helped develop the Stanford-Binet believed in eugenics—the selective breeding of human beings, much the same way that animal breeders work with champion stock. The eventual goal of eugenics was to create a better human race—smarter, stronger, healthier. That might not sound like such a bad goal, but assigning value to human beings based on some external quality is actually a very dangerous way to think. When Nazi Germany carried out this idea, the

Adolf Hitler believed that eugenics could be used to "purify" the human race; by killing the human beings he considered genetically "inferior," he planned to create a superior gene pool that would give birth to a "master race."

government killed humans deemed to be "inferior," including Jews, gypsies, homosexuals, children or adults who had mental retardation, and any individual with genetic defects.

American eugenicists may have not gone to such an extreme, but the concept of IQ was nevertheless used to support American discrimination and prejudice. Goddard, for example, used his IQ tests to determine that all immigrants except those from Northern Europe were of "surprisingly low intelligence": 87 percent of Russian immigrants were morons. Of course Goddard didn't take into account that these immigrants were being given a test in English, with questions based on American cultural assumptions, when they could barely, if at all, speak English. Goddard lobbied for more restrictive immigration policies, and vast numbers of immigrants were deported in 1913 and 1914 because of this test.

By the 1920s, Americans' use of the Stanford-Binet Scale and other tests had created a multimillion-dollar testing industry. In one year during the 1980s, teachers gave over 500 million standardized tests to children and adults across the United States. In 1989, the American Academy for the Advancement of Science listed the IQ test among the twenty most significant scientific discoveries of the century, along with nuclear fission, DNA, the transistor, and flight.

IQ tests still carried this message, however: a high score is good, a low score is bad. It qualified people according to their ability to respond to a set of questions that had little to do with kindness or integrity or any other moral value.

The human brain is a mysterious thing. No test will ever completely measure its abilities.

So What Do IQ Tests Actually Measure?

If an IQ test is supposed to measure a person's intelligence, the next question is: What is intelligence? Is it the ability to do well in school? Is it the ability to read well and spell correctly?

In the 1980s, a growing chorus of critics spoke out against IQ tests. For example, Yale psychologist Robert Sternberg said that psychologists know "almost nothing about what it is that they have been measuring. The tests have proved overall to have only low to moderate power to predict such things as future job performance, income and status, or overall happiness and adjustment." Linda S. Siegel, a professor in the Department of Educational Psychology and Special Education at the University of British Columbia in Vancouver, Canada, claims that IQ tests measure, for the most part, what a person has *learned*, not what he is capable of doing in the future (his potential).

Despite their many critics, however, IQ tests have become a fixture in North American education. Although we no longer use derogatory words like "moron" and "idiot" to speak of children, we still use the word "gifted"—which also implies a value judgment based on IQ. In reality, though, the concept of giftedness includes far more than just IQ.

Chapter 2
Ultimatum

Can you stay awake today?" my friend Maggie asked me as we put our coats in our lockers the next morning.

"Ha, ha," I said. Even though I'm friends with Maggie, we're not all that close. She's best friends with Kacy, and they make fun of me when I do really well on a test—and when I do really badly. My best friend, Sarah, moved away last year, and things haven't been the same since.

"It was so funny when you sat up with drool all over your face," she said.

"I did *not* drool." I would have noticed that.

The first class of the day was French. I'm actually pretty good at French, even though I mess up the grammar questions sometimes. When we started learning, there was a story in our French book, spread out with a little in each chapter, the words getting harder as the story went along. Have I mentioned that I read constantly? I love stories. So I wanted to know what the story was about and when we read the bit in the first chapter I wanted to know what happened next. I went home and tried to figure it out, using the big French dictionary I checked out of the library. Before long, I was learning about verbs and past tense and all that. Grammar isn't something I'd normally feel like bothering with, but you have to know it to understand French. I hate not understanding what something means. That's why I don't like math: there doesn't seem to be a reason for it, so I don't think it's worth bothering with.

Besides French, I'm also good at English. I can usually even do the grammar because I read so much. I do what looks right and generally it's the right answer. I used to be good at history and social studies, but that was before this year and Mr. Tepper. I'm not great at music, because I have what they call a tin ear. In art I get by, because you can do whatever, and as long as you make it sound artistic when you talk about it, the teachers are happy. It helps when we're working on clay, for example, if I frown at the clay a lot, then pinch it and poke it randomly. Finally, when the clay starts looking like something I can pretend to have intended, I start looking a little more satisfied as I pinch and poke, as though my vision is being realized.

Jason White sits in front of me in French. Rob Spanogle sits in front of him, and Hunter sits across the aisle from them. In the past, I used to stare past Jason's shoulder at Rob's back, looking at the one soft-looking curl in the middle of his neck. Today when I sat down, I looked at Hunter instead. He was looking at me and he smiled. I looked away quickly and stared at my desk. In the year I'd had a crush on Rob, he'd barely even noticed me. And then, when he did, it killed the crush. I wasn't sure what to do when a guy I liked actually smiled at me. Why? Why would Hunter like me anyway? I glanced back up at him and tried to smile casually before opening my French book and trying to focus on the paragraph explaining how Claude and Genevieve went shopping at *le magasin* for *le pain et le lait*.

Partway through French class, Hunter dropped his pen so that it rolled back toward my desk. Jason picked it up and handed it to him, and Hunter frowned. A minute later, he dropped the pen again, this time flicking it so that it went past my desk. Before anyone could move to get it for him, he jumped up and went to pick it up himself. He leaned on my desk as he bent to reach for the pen, and when he took his hand away there was a little piece of paper, about an inch square, lying on my desk.

I opened the note slowly, smoothing it out. It said: "A bunch of us are going to a movie Friday night and probably hanging out at Chicken Joe's afterward. Will you come with us?"

I sat very still for a moment, hardly breathing. He couldn't possibly have given the note to the wrong person after all the trouble he'd gone to with the pen. I had always been considered a geek and a brain, even though my grades weren't always great. None of the popular kids had ever bothered to notice me, since I was usually quiet and my friends and I stayed out of the way. But then I had fallen asleep in history class. Which made Rob Spanogle and his friends make fun of me in the library. Which annoyed me so that I gave them a sarcastic, mouthy answer. Which made Hunter smile at me and ask me out. Interesting. So falling asleep in class was really a good thing. I decided right then I'd better not mess up this chance to be popular.

I didn't try to write a note back to Hunter, mostly because I didn't think I could get it to him without being seen. Lunch was the first chance I had to talk to him. He stopped in front of me as we were both headed to different tables to sit down and looked questioningly at me. "Yes," I said, and his smile lit up his face.

"Great," he said. "We'll meet at the theater at eight." Then Rob and Jason showed up and he was gone, over at the popular table with his friends.

I sat with Maggie and Kacy, and ate my turkey sandwich in tiny bites. Today was Tuesday; how was I ever going to last until Friday?

"Are we going to hang out at my house this Friday?" Kacy asked. "My parents have a dinner thing they're going to, and they said we could order a pizza and rent some movies."

"Oh, good," Maggie said. "Let's get something scary."

I'd forgotten that Kacy had mentioned this yesterday. "I can't come," I said. "I have something else going on."

"What?" Maggie stared at me.

I shrugged. "Just something."

After supper that night, I went into Dad's study, where he was working on his computer, doing something for the furniture store he still managed.

"Dad," I said. "I have a date Friday night."

He frowned at me. "Have you talked to your mother about this?"

"No."

He pushed back his chair and stood up, then walked to the door and leaned into the hall. "Jody," he called, "will you come here for a minute?"

When Mom walked into the room, he said, "Ann tells me she has a date for this weekend."

"Aren't you a little young to be dating?" Mom asked.

"I'm fourteen."

Then they asked me all the questions parents are supposed to. Who was Hunter? What was he like? Where would we go? Would there be other people there? What time would I leave, and what time would I be home?

I had expected all those questions, but then Mom asked, "Don't you have a history test on Thursday?" Somehow, she always kept track of these things.

"Yes."

Mom and Dad looked at each other. "Okay," Dad said, "here's the deal: if you do well on your history test you may go. But we want you to take the cell phone for emergencies, and we want you to be home by eleven."

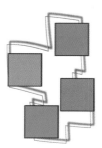

Definitions of "Gifted"

In Marland's 1971 report to Congress, he stated:

Children capable of high performance include those with demonstrated achievement and/or potential ability in any of the following areas, singly or in combination:

1. general intellectual ability

2. specific academic aptitude

3. creative or productive thinking

4. leadership ability

5. visual or performing arts

6. **psychomotor** ability

Using this broad definition of giftedness, most school systems identified between 10 and 15 percent of their students as "gifted and talented."

The U.S. Office of Gifted and Talented provides definitions for each of the six aspects of ability in relations to gifted students.

General Intellectual Ability or Talent

This is usually defined by a high score on some form of intelligence test, often referred to as an IQ test. Parents and teachers often recognize students with general intellectual talent by their wide-ranging fund of general information and high levels of vocabulary, memory, abstract word knowledge, and abstract reasoning.

Specific Academic Aptitude or Talent

Students with specific academic aptitudes are identified by their outstanding performance on an achievement or aptitude test in one area such as mathematics or language arts. The organizers of talent searches sponsored by a number of universities and colleges identify students with specific academic aptitude who score at the 97th percentile or higher on standard achievement tests and then give these students the Scholastic Aptitude Test (SAT). Remarkably large numbers of students score at these high levels.

Creative and Productive Thinking

This is the ability to produce new ideas by bringing together elements usually thought of as independent or unlike, and the aptitude for developing new meanings that have social value. Characteristics of creative and productive students include openness to experience, setting personal standards for evaluation, ability to play with ideas, willingness to take risks, preference for complexity, tolerance for *ambiguity*, positive self-image, and the ability to become totally absorbed by a task. Creative and productive students are identified through the use of tests such as the Torrance Test of Creative Thinking, or through demonstrated creative performance.

Leadership Ability

Leadership can be defined as the ability to direct individuals or groups to a common decision or action. Students who demonstrate giftedness in leadership

Creativity is the amazing human ability to produce something new—an idea, an invention, a work of art.

Leadership ability is a kind of giftedness that is quite different from academic intelligence. Being able to help a group work together to get things done is a special aptitude.

ability use group skills and negotiate in difficult situations. Many teachers recognize leadership through a student's keen interest and skill in problem solving. Leadership characteristics include self-confidence, responsibility, cooperation, a tendency to dominate, and the ability to adapt readily to new situations. These students can be identified through instruments such as the Fundamental Interpersonal Relations Orientation-Behavior (FIRO-B).

Visual and Performing Arts

Students with talent in the arts demonstrate special gifts in visual art, music, dance, drama, or other related studies. These students can be identified by using task descriptions such as the Creative Products Scales, which were developed for the Detroit Public Schools by Patrick Byrons and Beverly Ness Parke of Wayne State University.

Psychomotor Ability

This involves **kinesthetic** motor abilities such as practical, **spatial**, mechanical, and physical skills. In reality, it is seldom used as a **criterion** in educational programs for gifted students.

Other Perspectives on Students with Special Gifts

Mental Self-Management

Robert Sternberg and Robert Wagner (1982) have also suggested that giftedness is far more than merely intellectual abilities. They believe it requires a kind of mental self-management that includes three basic elements:

- adapting to environments
- selecting new environments
- shaping environments.

A person with special gifts is often able to find new solutions to problems.

According to Sternberg and Wagner, these elements are based on three main processes:

- separating relevant from irrelevant information

- combining isolated pieces of information into a unified whole

- relating newly acquired information to information acquired in the past

Sternberg and Wagner emphasize problem-solving abilities; they view the student with special gifts as one who processes information rapidly and uses insight and **intuition**. Howard Gardner (1983) also suggested a concept of multiple intelligences, stating that there are several ways of viewing the world: linguistic, logical/mathematical, spatial, musical, bodily-kinesthetic, interpersonal, and intrapersonal intelligence.

Fourteen Characteristics of a Child with Special Gifts

According to the Council for Exceptional Children, gifted children in general tend to possess fourteen characteristics, listed below. (These are typical characteristics, but no single child will be outstanding in all factors.)

1. Shows superior reasoning powers and marked ability to handle ideas; can generalize readily from specific facts and can see subtle rela-tionships; has outstanding problem-solving ability.

2. Shows persistent intellectual curiosity; asks searching questions; shows exceptional interest in the nature of human beings and the universe.

3. Has a wide range of interests, often of an intellectual kind; develops one or more interests to considerable depth.

4. Is markedly superior in quality and quantity of written and/or spoken vocabulary; is interested in the **subtleties** of words and their uses.

5. Reads avidly and absorbs books well beyond his or her years.

6. Learns quickly and easily and **retains** what is learned; recalls important details, concepts and principles; comprehends readily.

7. Shows insight into arithmetical problems that require careful reasoning and grasps mathematical concepts readily.

8. Shows creative ability or imaginative expression in such things as music, art, dance, and drama; shows sensitivity and **finesse** in rhythm, movement, and body control.

9. Sustains concentration for lengthy periods and shows outstanding responsibility and independence in classroom work.

10. Sets realistically high standards for self; is self-critical in evaluating and correcting his or her own efforts.

11. Shows *initiative* and originality in intellectual work; shows flexibility in thinking and considers problems from a number of viewpoints.

12. Observes keenly and is responsive to new ideas.

13. Shows social poise and an ability to communicate with adults in a mature way.

14. Gets excitement and pleasure from intellectual challenge; shows an alert and subtle sense of humor.

Ability, Motivation, and Creativity

Another expert in the field of gifted education, Joseph Renzulli, also believes that being gifted means more than intelligence alone. He defines "gifted behavior" as an interaction among three basic clusters of human traits:

- above-average general and/or specific abilities
- high levels of task commitment (motivation)
- high levels of creativity.

According to Renzulli, gifted and talented children are those who possess (or are capable of developing) this collection of traits—and then applying them to any potentially valuable area of human performance.

The concept of giftedness continues to be difficult to define. Many organizations, including the U.S. legal system, have their own definitions.

National Association for Gifted Children (NAGC) Definition

A gifted person is someone who shows, or has the potential for showing, an exceptional level of performance in one or more areas of expression.

Some of these abilities are very general and can affect a broad spectrum of the person's life, such as leadership skills or the ability to think creatively. Some are very specific talents and are only evident in particular circumstances, such as a special aptitude in mathematics, science, or music. The term giftedness provides a general reference to this spectrum of abilities without being specific or dependent on a single measure or index. It is generally recognized that approximately five percent of the student population, or three million children, in the United States are considered gifted.

A person's giftedness should not be confused with the means by which giftedness is observed or assessed. Parent, teacher, or student recommendations, a high mark on an examination, or a high IQ score are not giftedness; they may be a signal that giftedness exists. Some of these indices of giftedness are more sensitive than others to differences in the person's environment.

The Javits Act Definition

In 1988, the Javits Act provided grants for educational programs serving bright children from low-income families. It defined gifted according to these terms:

> The term gifted and talented student means children and youths who give evidence of higher performance capability in such areas as intellectual, creative, artistic, or leadership capacity, or in specific academic fields, and who require services or activities not ordinarily provided by the schools in order to develop such capabilities fully.

U.S. Office of Educational Research and Improvement (OERI) Definition

In a 1993 report titled *National Excellence and Developing Talent*, the term "gifted" was dropped. This definition uses the term "outstanding talent" and concludes with the sentence: "Outstanding talents are present in children and youth from all cultural groups, across all economic strata, and in all areas of human endeavor."

Chapter 3
History Test

I stared at the history test on my desk. I'd studied, really I had. I'd read both the chapters we were being tested on: the French Revolution and the Napoleonic Wars. The chapters in the book were very short, only about three pages each, with hardly any details. Mr. Tepper must have added stuff of his own, things I hadn't written down. I'd decided I'd better do some of my own research. I read the online encyclopedia entries for both the topics and all the entries on the people who looked important. Then I'd gotten distracted by a novel someone was working on about Josephine and Napoleon. I knew pretty much what everything was about—and a whole lot about Josephine's life as a child in Martinique—but apparently Mr. Tepper wasn't looking for a general understanding of the French Revolution and the Napoleonic Wars. He wanted details. All those details I didn't remember.

The test was divided into three parts: multiple choice, true or false, and fill in the blank. People usually said they liked this kind of test because it was easy, but for me it was hard. If Mr. Tepper had asked open-ended essay questions, I could have written down everything I knew and proved that I did know something. Instead, I had to figure out questions like, "What was the main cause of the French Revolution? (a) The success of the American Revolution, (b) The unequal class system, (c) The influence of Napoleon Bonaparte, or (d) Crop failures and the resulting food shortages." The *main* cause? The only thing I was sure of was that the answer wasn't c. The others had all contributed to the people's dissatisfaction. I circled b, but I still wasn't sure what Mr. Tepper wanted. This was probably something he'd written on the board—"The main cause of the French Revolution was _____." And everyone had written it down and then memorized it when they were studying. Except me, because I'd been working on a story about a girl who could fly, instead of taking notes.

The entire test was like that. I kept thinking more than one of the multiple-choice answers could be right, and whichever one was *most* right depended on how you thought about it. The true-or-false questions usually looked partly true and partly false, and I wasn't sure if a little bit false was enough to make the whole question false. I knew some of the fill-in-the-blank questions, as long as they were about names and not dates. I knew the general range of dates, but not the exact days.

After the test, I felt drained and exhausted. I'd studied for hours, but I wasn't sure it had done any good.

"How was your history test?" Mom asked as soon as I walked in the door.

"I don't know," I said. "Okay, I guess." Which wasn't true at all, but I didn't want to say that to Mom. I was hoping that somehow I had guessed right on most of the questions so my parents would never know I didn't have a clue.

Mr. Tepper always hands back tests during the next class. He has that kind of reputation. Of course, since he doesn't ask any essay questions, his tests are probably really easy to grade. If I'd been lucky, we wouldn't have had history again until Monday, and then I could have gone to the movies with Hunter without ever knowing how I did on the test. I wasn't lucky, though. History was the second class of the day on Friday.

As soon as we sat down, Mr. Tepper started handing back the test. He laid the paper upside down on my desk as he walked by. I sat there for a long moment before I dared to turn it over. Then I wished I hadn't. Circled in the corner was a big red F.

After that I couldn't pay attention. Mr. Tepper had started the next chapter and was talking about the Industrial Revolution, but all I could think of was what my parents were going to say and how this meant I couldn't go out with Hunter that night. And I had never failed anything in my life before. What did this mean for the rest of my life? That I'd peaked somewhere in elementary school and my mind was now descending into oblivion, like Charlie in *Flowers for Algernon?*

When I got home that afternoon, I tried to sneak into the house without being seen. I crept up to my room and silently pushed open the door, only to discover that Mom was sitting on my bed waiting for me.

"How did you do on your history test?"

I just shrugged and dropped my backpack on the floor. I couldn't think of anything good to say to her. I sat down at my desk and turned on my computer.

Mom sighed. "Mr. Tepper called me, but I wanted to give you a chance to tell me about it yourself. You can't ignore this, Ann. Things are going to change. You have to realize there are consequences to your actions—starting with the fact that you will not be going out with that boy this evening."

I'd known they were going to say that, of course, but maybe I'd hoped they'd be nice and understanding. I stared at the computer screen and a lump clogged my throat, getting bigger and bigger. The screen blurred. I bit my lip as the tears started to overflow and spill down my cheeks.

I didn't want Mom to notice I was crying, but she did, of course. "Ann," she said, a little more gently, "I love you and I want the best for you. You can do so much better than this."

When Dad got home, he said pretty much the same things as Mom, only more angrily. He promised to have a family meeting after supper about my future, but then he had to leave again because of some kind of inventory emergency at the store.

Maybe Mom was feeling sorry for me after all, because she let me take a sandwich up to my room for supper, instead of having to face her and Daniel at the table. While I was nibbling at the sandwich and clicking randomly around the Internet, I had an idea. Dad wouldn't be home until at least midnight, which meant there would be no family meeting tonight. If I locked the door of my room and climbed out the window, I could go out with Hunter and be back before anyone realized I was gone. If Mom happened to come up to my room, she would just think I was asleep or upset.

I felt much better after I made this decision. My life wasn't going all that well, but maybe Hunter would be my boyfriend and things would change. I quickly got dressed, and then slid the window open. I ducked out onto the roof of the back porch and walked to the far end, where

the big tree hung close to the house. I'd planned on grab-
bing a branch and kind of swinging down onto the porch,
or maybe doing hand over hand to the tree trunk. What
actually happened was that, first of all, I had to jump for the
branch because it wasn't as close as I'd anticipated. I scraped
my palms, but managed to hang on. I dangled there, realiz-
ing I wasn't going to be able to reach the porch from where
I was. Then my hands started slipping, and I tried to shift
into a lower position. Instead, I fell, dropping nearly four
feet to the ground and rolling when I landed. The knees of
my pants were scuffed and dirty and my hands were bleed-
ing a bit, but I was free.

A shiver of exhilaration went down my spine. I wondered if this was how slaves had felt when they finally made
a break for the North and started on the Underground
Railroad. Or how the von Trapp family had felt when they
crossed the Alps into Switzerland, leaving the Nazis behind.

I made it to the movie theater a couple of minutes
before eight. It took me a while to spot Hunter amid the
crowds of teenagers. He was standing with Rob and Jason
and Brenna Murphy and Tirza Kay, a couple of the popular
girls. When Hunter saw me, his face lit up and he beckoned
me over. The others took a few seconds longer to notice me,
but when they did, they looked surprised.

"What are *you* doing here?" Tirza asked.

"I invited her," Hunter said, before I could say anything.

"Why?" Rob looked confused.

"Because she seemed funny and nice." Hunter sounded defensive, and he was starting to look confused himself.

The evening I had been looking forward to all week went downhill quickly. No one except Hunter talked to me, and even Hunter seemed quiet and troubled. He was nice to me, bought me popcorn and a drink, and whispered a few comments during the movie, but everything felt ruined. From time to time, Hunter had long whispered conversations with Jason, who sat on his other side. I couldn't hear what they said, and I wasn't sure I wanted to. I had expected the others to accept me simply because Hunter did, and he apparently had expected the same thing. Instead, I seemed to be some horrible social blunder that Hunter had made.

I didn't pay much attention to the movie. There was a lot of machine-gun fire and improbable stunts, but I had no idea what the plot was supposed to be. Plot was the kind of thing I *always* cared about, but this time I was too miserable.

When the movie let out, we all stood around awkwardly on the sidewalk outside the theater. Tirza and Brenna were giggling and nudging each other. I didn't wait for Hunter to tell me to leave. "I've got to get home," I said. "My family's leaving at five A.M. to drive to my grandma's house, and I want to get a couple of hours of sleep before we go."

It was a total lie, but Hunter looked relieved and unhappy at the same time. "I'll see you around," he said.

At home, I discovered two bad things. The first was that my father's car was in the driveway. The second was that I couldn't figure out how to get back onto the porch roof. I was standing on the railing, clinging to the eaves trough, when the porch light came on. I froze. I heard the doorknob rattle as it turned and the slight squeak of the door as it opened.

"Ann," said my father's voice. "Get down from there right now."

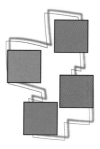

The History of Giftedness

Down through the ages, humanity has recognized and celebrated people with exceptional abilities. In the nineteenth century, however, the notion of "gifted" first came into being as an educational concept, and it has continued to develop since then.

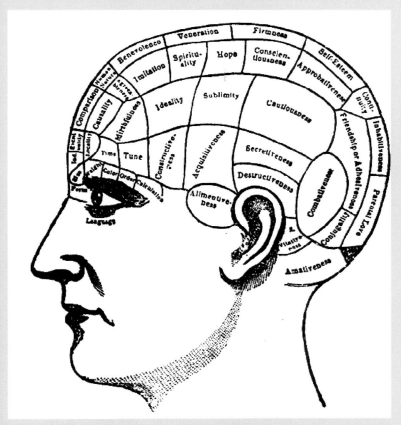

Early in the nineteenth century, scientists believed that intelligence and character could be assessed by studying the shape of a person's head according to this map. As the century progressed, however, they turned their attention to other methods of assessing intelligence.

A Time Line of Key Dates in Gifted and Talented Education

1868   William Torrey Harris, superintendent of public schools for St. Louis, institutes the earliest systematic efforts in public schools to educate students who are gifted.

1869   Francis Galton's *Hereditary Genius* is published, indicating that intelligence was passed through successive generations. His biographical study of over four hundred British men throughout history led him to conclude through statistical methods that intelligence was derived from heredity and natural selection.

1901   Worster, Massachusetts, opens the first special school for children who are gifted.

1905   French researchers, Binet and Simon, develop a series of tests to identify children of inferior intelligence for the purpose of separating them from normally functioning children for placement in special classrooms. Their notion of mental age revolutionizes the science of psychological testing by capturing intelligence in a single numerical outcome.

1908   Henry Goddard translates Binet's test into English and passes it on to American educators and psychologists.

1916   Lewis Terman, the "father" of the gifted education movement, publishes the Stanford-Binet Intelligence Scale, forever changing intelligence testing and the face of American education.

1917   The United States' entry into World War I necessitates the mobilization of a large-scale army. The Army Alpha and Beta tests were created and administered to over one million recruits, making intelligence testing seem still more useful and accurate in the eyes of both educators and the general public.

1918   Lulu Stedman establishes an "opportunity room" for students who were gifted within the University Training School at the Southern Branch of the University of California.

1921   Lewis Terman begins what has remained the longest running **longitudinal** study of children who are gifted with an original sample of 1,500 gifted children.

1922   Leta S. Hollingworth begins the Special Opportunity Class at P.S. 165 in New York City for students who were gifted. This class would yield nearly forty research articles and a textbook.

1925   Lewis Terman publishes *Genetic Studies of Genius*, concluding that students who are gifted were: (a) qualitatively different in school, (b) slightly better physically and emotionally in comparison to typical students, (c) superior in academic subjects in comparison to the average students, (d) emotionally stable, (e) most successful when education and family values were held in high regard by the family, and (f) infinitely variable in combination with the number of traits exhibited by those in the study. This is the first volume in a five-volume study spanning nearly forty years.

1926   Leta Hollingworth publishes *Gifted Child: Their Nature and Nurture*, which is considered to be the first textbook on gifted education.

1936   Hollingworth establishes P.S. 500, the Speyer School, for children who were gifted, ages seven through nine.

1950   National Science Foundation Act provides federal support for research and education in mathematics, physical sciences, and engineering.

1954   The National Association of Gifted Children is founded under the leadership of Ann Isaacs. *Brown vs. The Board of Education* ends "separate but equal education."

1957   The Soviet Union launches **Sputnik**, sparking the United States to reexamine its human capital and quality of American schooling, particularly in mathematics and science. As a result, substantial amounts of money pour into identifying the brightest and talented students who would best profit from advanced math, science, and technology programs.

1958   The National Defense Education Act passes, the first large-scale effort by the federal government in gifted education.

1964   The Civil Rights Act passes, emphasizing equal opportunities for all, including those in education.

1972   The Marland Report is the first formal definition encouraging schools to define giftedness broadly; along with academic and intellectual talent the definition includes leadership ability, visual and performing arts, creative or productive thinking, and psychomotor ability.

Governments have come to realize that human intelligence and other talents are national resources that can be utilized to build a country's strength.

1974   The Office of the Gifted and Talented housed within the U.S. Office of Education is given official status.

1983   The government publication *A Nation at Risk* reports the scores of America's brightest students and their failure to compete with international counterparts. The report includes policies and practices for gifted education, raising academic standards, and promoting appropriate curriculum for gifted learners.

1988   Congress passes the Jacob Javits Gifted and Talented Students Education Act as part of the Reauthorization of the Elementary and Secondary Education Act.

1990   National Research Centers on the Gifted and Talented are established at the University of Connecticut, University of Virginia, Yale University, and Northwestern University

1993   *National Excellence: The Case for Developing America's Talent* is issued by the United States Department of Education, outlining how America neglects its most talented youth. The report also makes a number of recommendations influencing the next decade of research in the field of gifted education.

1998   The National Association for Gifted Children publishes *Pre-K–Grade 12 Gifted Program Standards* to provide guidance in seven key areas for programs serving gifted and talented students.

2002　The No Child Left Behind Act (NCLB) is passed as the reauthorization of the Elementary and Secondary Education Act. The Javits program is included in NCLB, and expanded to offer competitive statewide grants. The definition of students who are gifted and talented is modified again: *"Students, children, or youth who give evidence of high achievement capability in areas such as intellectual, creative, artistic, or leadership capacity, or in specific academic fields, and who need services and activities not ordinarily provided by the school in order to fully develop those capabilities."*

2004　*A Nation Deceived: How Schools Hold Back America's Brightest Students*, a national research-based report on acceleration strategies for advanced learners, is published by the Belin-Blank Center at the University of Iowa.

Chapter 4
Grounded

After the sneaking-out incident—or, more exactly, the getting-caught incident—I was, of course, grounded for two months. I barely cared, at least about the evenings. The date with Hunter had been a fiasco. He hadn't spoken to me since and had only given me a few embarrassed glances.

Worse than the grounding, my parents had taken my computer out of my room. That computer had been my lifeline. I tried to explain to them that my online friends were counting on me to help them write code for our game and that they'd be worried about me when I suddenly stopped showing up. Mom and Dad said they didn't see how they could really be my friends when I'd never even met them in real life. So my computer sat on a side table in the dining room, the Internet disabled. If I needed to write a paper, I had to write it there, where Mom and Dad could drift by every once in a while and see that I was really working.

I hated my life. I felt like a stupid loser—although ironically my nickname in school was still "the brain." I had no real friends; Maggie and Kacy had reacted with disbelief when I told them what had happened, and they still suspected I was lying. I couldn't use the Internet. I couldn't even go to the library and curl up with a book anymore, since Mom and Dad had made it clear that I had to come straight home after school. Even when the two months were up, I didn't think anything wonderful could happen that would make my life much better.

A week after I got the history test back, Mr. Tepper walked up to my desk at the beginning of class and bent down. "I've made an appointment for you with the guidance counselor at 9:30 today," he said in a low voice. I could feel everyone looking at me, and, out of the corner of my eye, I saw heads bent together, whispering.

At 9:25, I got up and walked out of the room without asking. Mr. Tepper knew where I was going, so I decided I didn't need to get permission.

The guidance counselor was Mrs. Moss. I'd never been to her office, but I knew where it was. When I got there,

Mrs. Moss was sitting behind her desk, looking at a file. "Come in," she said. "Shut the door and have a seat."

After I sat down, she leaned back in her chair and looked at me. "You're an extremely intelligent girl, Ann. I've just been reading your file. But Mr. Tepper tells me you've been having some trouble in his class. Do you want to tell me what went wrong with this test you took last week?"

"It was a stupid test."

"Did you study?".

"Yes, I studied," I said indignantly. "I spent hours studying."

"Then what happened?"

"It was a stupid test," I said again. "Have you seen it?"

Mrs. Moss ignored my question. "Mr. Tepper gave me a list of the class's grades for the test. Most students got a B or a C, a few got A's. There was only one F—yours. What does that tell you?"

"That I'm the stupidest person in my class?" I felt sick.

The guidance counselor gave me a look. "Since your IQ scores suggest otherwise, the only conclusion I can make is that you are not trying. Perhaps because you know you're smart, you think you don't have to pay attention or study."

"How can that be the only conclusion? I did try. I told you I studied for hours. Clearly, there has to be another conclusion." I was getting more and more frustrated.

"If you had tried hard enough, you would have done well on the test. This is not an ability problem."

"I did study," I said, "whatever you think. But I don't know why I should even bother. I don't care about this stuff. There are lots of interesting things we could be talking about in class, but why does it matter when someone did whatever? Why should I have to be able to read Mr. Tepper's mind and learn to think like him? Aren't we supposed to be learning to think for ourselves?"

This was probably one of those times when I should have kept my mouth shut. I was upset and near tears; I was not having a good life this week.

Mrs. Moss clearly thought I should have kept my mouth shut, too. "You will speak to me with more respect," she said. "Mr. Tepper is a good teacher, teaching the best way he knows how. Just because you would prefer someone else doesn't make you right." And then she called my parents.

That night we had another family meeting.

"What are you thinking, Ann?" Dad asked. "I don't know who you are anymore. You fail tests, sneak out of the house, and you're disrespectful to your teachers."

I couldn't think of anything to say that wouldn't make things worse.

"I guess being smart isn't everything," Mom said. "Look at you and Daniel: just as smart, being raised in the same home, going to the same school, but he's getting straight A's and you're barely passing."

I started to cry. Hot tears poured down my face, making it hard to breathe. My ears and nose and throat all ached. "Do you really love Daniel more than you love me?" I choked.

Mom shook her head impatiently. "Don't try to make this about something else."

The outcome of the whole horrible conversation was that I was now grounded for three months instead of two.

For the next few months I tried to be good and do well in school. I didn't write stories in class anymore, and I tried to pay attention. It didn't always work, though. Mr. Tepper was just so completely boring that my mind would seize on the few interesting things he would say and run away with them. Maybe he'd say something like, "The coal smoke would mix with the river vapor, leading to the famous London fogs, thick and dirty and greasy." Then I would realize, five or fifteen or forty minutes later, I'd been off in a daydream, imagining creeping blindly through the filthy fog while cutthroats prowled in unseen doorways. It was hard to pay attention when I really didn't care what he was saying.

Life went on like this for a while. I wasn't very happy, but I got used to doing my homework in the dining room and not going to the library. I survived by reading all the books I owned over and over again and by planning out elaborate stories in my head. I'd always done that, but now they became a bigger part of my everyday life.

Then, one day in late January, only a couple of weeks after my grounding finally ended, Dad called another family meeting. I didn't think I'd done anything to get yelled at about this time, but I wasn't completely sure, so I was nervous when we all sat down in the living room together. Dad looked pale and jumpy. At first I thought that was bad, but when he spoke, I realized he was excited.

"Last fall I applied for a job opening inside the company," he said. "District manager of six stores. I had an interview last month and I hadn't heard anything, so I assumed they'd hired someone else. But today they called me and offered me the position."

"Wow, Dad, that's great," Daniel said. "Congratulations."

"Yeah," I said. "Good for you. When do you start?"

"I start next week," Dad said, and then paused. "There's something else. The job is in Maddox, about twelve hours away. We'll have to move."

The Challenges of Being Gifted

Self-Esteem Issues

Often the products of a child's special mental capacities are valued—while the traits that come with those capacities are not. For example, winning an essay contest on the dangers of global warming may get a student lots of attention and praise, but her intense emotional reaction to the threat technology poses to the planet and its life forms may be considered excessive, overly dramatic, even neurotic. If she tries to act on her beliefs by going on strike to force her family or school to renounce what she considers harmful technology, she may be ridiculed, scolded, or even punished. Writing a winning essay is deemed not only okay but admirable; being the sort of person she had to be to write it may not be considered okay with those around her.

When teachers and parents focus only on what young people with special gifts can do rather than on who they are, they ignore vital aspects of their developing identities. In 1991, to help counteract the growing focus on achievement, the Columbus Group, a group of theorists, practitioners, and parents, suggested a new definition of giftedness in children:

Giftedness is *asynchronous* development in which advanced cognitive abilities and heightened intensity combine to create inner experiences and awareness that are qualitatively different from the norm. This asynchrony increases with higher intellectual capacity. The uniqueness of the gifted renders them particularly vulnerable and requires modifications in parenting, teaching, and counseling in order for them to develop optimally.

This view suggests that children with special gifts develop differently from other kids. They may reach recognized developmental milestones on a schedule that is unique to them, putting them out of sync with society's expectations. In addition, they may be out of sync internally, with cognitive, social, and emotional development on separate and sometimes quite different timetables.

Individuals with special gifts often do not conform to the crowd. This may make others uncomfortable—but it also means that these individuals may offer new ideas and productive solutions to the rest of the human community.

This variability in behavior and perception is often difficult for parents and schools to handle—and difficult for the child as well. For example, the winner of the global warming essay contest may go on to have a successful career as an environmental lawyer. Or she may condemn herself for her intense emotional responses, just as her family and others condemned her. She may choose to shut down as best she can the aspects of herself that do not conform easily to society's expectations, and in doing so, also shut down important aspects of the energy that drives her. Understanding and support from parents and teachers make it possible for a child to develop not only her ability to get good grades, win awards, and move ahead on the career path she chooses, but to feel comfortable with herself and valuable as a person.

Common Issues Faced by Teens with Special Gifts

Perfection Issues

Adolescents who have special talents are often perfectionists, demanding only the best of themselves. Their standards may be set so high that they become discouraged with themselves, no matter how high their achievement may actually be.

Control Issues

Adolescents with special gifts often insist on complete control over their lives. This can lead to conflict with authority figures—and it can also combine with their perfectionism to make it difficult for them to take risks. Because they understand the possible consequences of actions better than many young people their age, they may become paralyzed by what "might" happen.

Expectation Issues

Many kids with special gifts experience the "push-pull" of what they want and what others want of them. They do not want to fall short of others' expectations, but when this issue blends with their need for both perfection and control, they may become either paralyzed—or believe they have to prove themselves again and again, living their lives under the constant pressure to succeed. This attitude can ultimately hurt their creativity and even squelch the very gifts that make these young people special.

Impatience Issues

Like most teens, adolescents with special gifts have little patience for either *ambiguity* or the need to wait for something (whether a relationship or a talent) to come to fruition. Some of these kids are naturally impulsive, yet this can work against them, making them seem immature at times. Most need to learn the necessity of investing time, whether it is in friendships, schoolwork, outside commitments, or their own development.

Identity Issues

Kids with special talents may be able to achieve at an adult level—but this does not necessarily mean that their emotional development is at the same stage of development. When these young people are pushed too fast along educational paths or careers that do allow them the time or opportunities to express adolescence's normal identity crises, they may experience dissatisfaction or frustration later in life.

Problems Encountered by Kids with Special Gifts

1. Perfectionism can lead to fear of failure, in turn causing a teen with special gifts to avoid failure by refusing to even try something (including homework assignments).

2. Keen observation, imagination, and ability to see beyond the obvious can cause a child who is gifted to appear shy, holding back in new situations in order to consider all the implications.

3. These young adults may require full details before answering questions or offering help, once again making them appear socially withdrawn.

4. Intense sensitivity can cause these adolescents to take criticism very personally. Normal interpersonal slights do not roll off their backs.

5. Sensitivity and a well-developed sense of right and wrong can lead these teens to intense concern over wars, starving children, pollution, and other forms of injustice and violence. If they are overloaded with images and discussions of these issues, they can become introverted and withdrawn or even suffer from depression.

6. Asynchronous development allows these young people to intellectually understand abstract concepts but be unable to deal with those concepts emotionally, leading to intense concerns about death, the future, sex, and other such issues.

7. Asynchronous development can also result in frustration when the young person's physical development leads to an inability to complete a task she is capable of intellectually envisioning. (Perfectionism may play a role in this frustration as well.)

8. Asynchronous development also causes a young teen with special gifts to be able to participate in adult conversations about issues such as global warming or world hunger one minute and the next minute cry and whine because he can't have his own way.

9. Advanced verbal and reasoning abilities can lead these young adolescents to be argumentative and/or manipulative. Parents and other adults need to remember that although credit should be given for logical and convincing arguments, a child is still a child and requires appropriate discipline, no matter how clever or cute the behavior may look. Young people who see they can manipulate adults may ultimately feel very insecure.

10. Advanced verbal and reasoning abilities can lead a teen with special talents to try to outsmart parents and teachers. It may also contribute to a sense of arrogance.

11. Sophisticated vocabulary and an advanced sense of humor can cause these teens to be misunderstood, which can make them feel inferior and rejected. (This is one reason young adults with special gifts often prefer to be around adults.)

What the Research Says

According to a recent study, students with exceptionally high special gifts may be at risk for problems in social and emotional development. To discover if peer relations are affected by type and/or amount of giftedness, extremely mathematically or verbally talented thirteen-year-olds (top 1 in 10,000) were compared to students who were modestly gifted (top 1 in 20) of similar age on measures of popularity and peer acceptance, participation in group activities, and personality traits. The verbally or mathematically talented students were also contrasted on the same measures. Virtually no differences in group activities or personality traits were found. In their ratings of peer perceptions, however, the modestly gifted group exceeded the extremely gifted, especially the verbally gifted, in social standing (as indicated by their ratings as "athletic" or "popular"). The students who were modestly gifted also rated themselves as more **extroverted**, socially adept, and uninhibited. Perceptions of peer ratings of importance and acceptance were higher for the mathematically than the verbally gifted. This study indicates that extremely **precocious** adolescents, especially the verbally precocious, may be at greater risk for developing problems in peer relations than modestly gifted youth.

Chapter 5
Goodbye, Mill Creek

Three weeks later, the moving truck was nearly packed and ready to go. Dad had already been living in a suburb of Maddox for a couple of weeks. We had all flown out one weekend and looked at houses, and Mom had fallen in love with a white three-bedroom with a fireplace and a picket fence. Dad was apparently camped out there now, sleeping on the floor of the master bedroom while he waited for our stuff to arrive.

I had mixed feelings about moving. I'd never lived anywhere except Mill Creek, but recently it had become less and less appealing. Sure, there were the nostalgic spots, like the comfy chairs in the library and the apple tree Sarah and

I had loved to climb when we were kids. I'd miss my bedroom, too, which was a decorating work in progress. Two walls were blue, one was green, and one had been a gigantic collage of photos, postcards, magazine pictures, and even a few poems and stories. (I'd had to take down the collage.) I'd hung a huge, fringy scarf from the ceiling over my bed. My parents didn't exactly love my room, but at least they'd pretty much let me do what I wanted with it.

The good part about moving would be getting to start over without anyone knowing who I was supposed to be. I probably wouldn't have cared about that if I'd been having a better year, though. I could start a new school—which was still scary—and no one would call me "brain." I could blend in quietly with the normal kids, sometimes passing, sometimes failing, and no one would know any different. And there would be no Mr. Tepper.

Daniel had been pretty cranky and surly since Dad told us we'd be moving. He really wasn't happy about leaving our school and his friends, which is one of the problems with being happy and popular. While we drove to Maddox, he sat in the front seat with his headphones on for almost the entire trip, glaring out the window and refusing to talk to anyone.

My room in the new house is the smallest bedroom. I don't care about that, but it looked so shabby and depressing when I first saw it that I wanted to cry. The walls were boring white and the carpet was drab beige. The bare window looked out over the snow-covered backyard. After we'd unloaded the truck, the room was a lot fuller, but just as depressing. Boxes were stacked around, and the furniture was stuck here and there. I threw my pillow and blankets on the mattress, curled up like a bird in a nest, and went to sleep.

The day after we got to Maddox, Daniel and I had to start school. I thought we should take a week off to settle in—or at least a day—but Mom kept saying things like, "There's no point in putting it off," and, "You don't want to get behind in your work." I didn't care if I was behind in the work. That would be normal, right?

Dad had apparently already registered us at the school, so the principal was expecting us when we walked in, half an hour before classes started. He was a youngish black man named Mr. Elkins, wearing a leather sport coat over a dark gray pullover.

"Daniel," Mr. Elkins said, "I understand you play basketball. We have an excellent team here. I've talked to Coach Schuster and he wants you to stop by and talk to him after school." Daniel started looking happier. I rolled my eyes.

Mr. Elkins looked at me and smiled. I wasn't sure whether he'd caught the eye roll or not. "Your father didn't mention any activities you were involved with back in Mill Creek, Ann," he said, "but we have quite a few extracurricular groups that you might be interested in. Why don't you look this list over and see what stands out to you?" He handed me a two-page printout, stapled in the corner. "Not that you want to get involved with too many things at once," he added.

I glanced down at the list—drama, chess, robotics, student council, band, a huge variety of sports—it went on and on. In Mill Creek, extracurricular activities had been either sports or band, or the yearbook if you were a senior.

After that, Mom went home, and Mr. Elkins took Daniel and me around to our classes. He explained to us how the school had half-hour homeroom periods at the beginning of each day, with the homeroom teacher acting as a kind of adviser to their students. Daniel would be in Ms. Namioka's class, and I would be in Ms. Atwood's. Our class schedules had been arranged to be as close as possible to what they had been in Mill Creek.

We took Daniel to his room first, and I stood in the hall while the principal took him in and introduced him. I listened to the murmur of the kids inside. I was not looking forward to my turn at all. Mr. Elkins came out lead me down the hall. My heart started to race, and my hands turned icy and sweaty.

"Are you feeling nervous?" Mr. Elkins asked, looking sideways at me. Probably he could hear how fast I was breathing.

"Um, maybe a little."

"I understand that you were having a few problems at your last school."

Oh great. Like that was supposed to make me less nervous.

"Don't worry," he said. "Ms. Atwood is a great teacher. She'll also be your history teacher. I'm sure you'll like her."

"Sure." Of course, history. That was just great.

We stopped at another door, and Mr. Elkins put his hand on the doorknob. "This is it."

When I first walked into the class, I had the impression of a sea of faces, all staring at me. Then I calmed down a tiny bit and realized there were really fewer people here than in my class back in Mill Creek—maybe only fifteen or so students, compared to the twenty-six in my class back home. Their desks were pushed into a rough semicircle, staggered so that some were further forward than others.

"You must be Ann," the teacher—Ms. Atwood—said, turning toward me with a smile. She was tall, with long red hair in a braid down her back.

"This is Ann Palliser," Mr. Elkins said to the class. "She and her brother just moved to town. Treat her well." He smiled at me. "I'll leave you in Ms. Atwood's capable hands."

"Why don't you take a seat over there, Ann." Ms. Atwood pointed to an empty desk on one side of the class, near a window. The girl in the next desk smiled at me as I sat down.

My first class of the day was history and I was in the same room. The class was talking about World War I. We'd been doing World War I back in Mill Creek, too, even though we'd had different books. Ms. Atwood, however, was a very different teacher from Mr. Tepper.

"Chris," she asked a guy on the other side of the room, "we've read about how whole classes of English schoolboys would graduate and enlist in the army together. What do you think made them want to do that?"

The question actually interested me, and, amazingly, Chris answered it. "They thought it was cool," he said. "Everybody kept telling them how great their country was and how they should fight for it, like war was a big basketball game or something that they could help win."

Ms. Atwood was nodding, as though Chris had said something she hadn't thought of before. "Why do you think they believed that?"

"They had all that propaganda stuff," a girl near me said.

"And it was like those poems we read," another girl jumped in, "where everyone said how great war was and then they got there and it was awful."

Huh, I thought. Maybe this school really would be okay.

Educational Programs for Children Who Are Gifted

Kids like Ann get frustrated and bored in school. Some educational settings may never even recognize that a student has special gifts; instead, he'll be like a square peg in a round hole, never managing to "fit" himself into his school's requirements. As a result, his special abilities will be seen as failures rather than gifts.

Many schools, however, have created special programs for kids who are gifted. Since the first use of the term "gifted," schools have used three major approaches for this group of students: acceleration, enrichment, and differentiation.

A person who's a "square peg" may have difficulty in world where everyone else is "round."

Acceleration

Acceleration means simply accelerating the educational process: speeding up a student's progression through the grades, so that a ten-year-old might be in high school, and a thirteen-year-old might graduate and go on to college. Some people are still in favor of this approach, while others do not believe it is beneficial to the total child who is being accelerated.

Why should students be accelerated?

There are two major reasons for accelerating students:

1. Students are accelerated in order to provide them with a learning environment in which others are working at a similar academic level.

2. Students are accelerated in order to streamline and shorten their course of study by one or more years. This enables accelerated students to move on from high school to further academic endeavors, internships, employment, or other life experiences sooner than they would have otherwise.

Acceleration moves a student with special gifts ahead of her classmates.

What are some factors to think about when considering acceleration?

The decision to accelerate should take into account the student's academic, physical, and social maturity. According to authors Dauber and Benbow, from the National Association for Gifted Children, the following guidelines should apply:

1. The student should be performing several grades above age level. When grade skipping is being considered, the child's performance should be advanced in several subject areas. (In other words, a six-year-old who reads at an eighth-grade level but is performing at grade level in mathematics, social studies, and science would not be considered an appropriate candidate for acceleration.)

2. The student should be socially and emotionally mature, so that she will be able to adjust to new settings and more mature peers.

3. When considering grade skipping, the student's physical size should be considered only to the extent that competitive sports may be viewed as important.

4. The student should be eager to move forward in school. He may be bored and unchallenged with the current curriculum and school setting.

Some research indicates that acceleration can be one of the best methods to meet the needs of students who are gifted. By skipping grades, these students may be grouped with other students with whom they have more in common, while they have the opportunity to do more challenging schoolwork.

However, not everyone agrees. Some parents, schools, and experts believe that accelerating students ignores their emotional needs. Because an eleven-year-old can do high-school level schoolwork, does

Enrichment offers special experiences and learning opportunities to students who are gifted. Some educators and parents question whether it is fair to give special "riches" to some students while excluding others.

not mean that child has the social skills necessary to navigate high school!

According to experts such as Susan Assouline and Nick Colangelo, who have developed the Iowa Acceleration Scale, a tool to help parents and educators make such decisions, acceleration should not be a general policy for students who are gifted; instead, it should be considered on a child-by-child basis. For example, acceleration may not be right for a high-school student who is also a star football player—or for one who isn't socially mature. Others may do better with acceleration in only one subject area, since many gifted children develop asynchronously.

Enrichment

Many experts believe that merely skipping grades is not the right approach for students with special gifts. Instead, experts like Joseph Renzulli advocate enrichment opportunities for these young people. "It's not just how far and fast one can run," he explains, "but rather what one can do to apply the material that one has learned in an environment that allows them to generate hypotheses, gather data, to write a play, poem or song."

Most enrichment programs are pull-out activities; the student attends regular classes most of the time, but is pulled out (usually once a week, but sometimes once a day or even once a month) for special classes that are more challenging. While some experts feel this is a good compromise for students with special talents, allowing them to benefit from "normal"

Whether schools apply the philosophy of acceleration, enrichment, or curriculum differentiation, the goal is to help students with special gifts rise to their full potentials.

social opportunities, while enriching their academic experiences, others complain that enrichment programs are elitist. In other words, it gives special privileges to a select few.

Educators who hold this perspective ask, Why shouldn't all students get the creative activities, field trips, in-depth studies, and hands-on puzzles that characterize pull-out enrichment programs? Why should students who are gifted be spared the monotony of "regular" classroom activities? After all, these are students who generally excel at school anyway. Why punish other students by making them sit through endless repetitions and seatwork assignments, while students who are gifted are rewarded with "fun" schoolwork?

Because of these criticisms, some educators encourage another approach that seems to be fairer to all students, whatever their gifts and talents.

Curriculum Differentiation

Curriculum differentiation seeks to tailor teaching environments and practices to create different learning experiences for different students.

Chapter 6
Discovering My Options

The first week of classes went by, slowly at first because I was still figuring out my way around and getting used to things, but picking up speed as I started to fit back into my niche—the niche where I do whatever I think is interesting and don't bother about the rest. History was much better than it had been with Mr. Tepper, but everything else was about the same.

Daniel, of course, loved the new school, even though he'd been the one moping around because we were leaving Mill Creek. Coach Schuster had already given him a tryout and put him on the basketball team. He'd made a ton of friends and even had a date on our first Friday night in Maddox.

I'd started eating lunch with Priya, the girl who sat next to me in homeroom, and her friend Liz. We didn't know each other very well yet, but we were slowly becoming friends—although none of us seemed to move at the friend-making speed of Daniel.

On Tuesday of my second week in Maddox, our homeroom class was listening to music and writing in our journals when Ms. Atwood called me up to her desk and had me sit in a chair next to her.

"How are you doing getting used to the new school, Ann?"

I looked over at the students, but none of them were looking at me. Ms. Atwood saw the look. "I conference with students now and then; everyone's used to it. They're not listening."

I shrugged. "I'm doing okay."

"It's always an adjustment, starting a new school in the middle of the year," she said. "The classes are never exactly the same as your old school, and you have the added pressure of trying to make new friends. I've been keeping an eye on you this past week," she went on, "and I've talked to your teachers to see how you're fitting in. I know it's early, but I want to make sure you have the best experience possible here. Tell me, did you read the student handbook?"

I looked at her blankly.

"It was in the packet of information and forms we gave your father."

Oh. I kind of remembered Dad handing me a bunch of papers. I thought maybe I had put them on top of my dresser. And, of course, immediately forgotten about them. "I'm not sure," I said, which wasn't at all true since I was absolutely positive I had *not* read it.

"This school believes in helping all our students reach their full potential," she said. "We want to help you learn to think critically and give you the skills to reach your goals."

"That's good." I wondered where she was going with this.

"For example," she said. "If I give you an assignment and you think it sounds boring, you have the right to come up with an alternate assignment. If I agree that your idea would cover the same types of ideas as the original assignment, I would let you go ahead."

"Really?" I stared at her. "But what if I wanted to do something really easy?"

"If I thought it was too easy I might help you come up with some ways to make it a more challenging project. Too easy is just as bad as too hard. We want to challenge all our students but not overwhelm them. Do you think you are being challenged?"

"I don't know." I hadn't thought about it.

"Do you think you were challenged at your last school?"

I shrugged. "I did okay on some stuff and not on others. I was failing history," I added.

She nodded. "Yes, I noticed that on your transcript. Why do you think that was?"

"I tried," I said, "but I just couldn't do the tests." I told her about the test I had failed and how I couldn't tell which answer Mr. Tepper wanted to the multiple-choice and true-or-false questions, even though I had studied.

"I don't give many multiple-choice tests," she said, looking thoughtful, "because I have found there are always a few students who have problems with them like you've described. That type of test isn't always very accurate unless you make the questions very easy, although some subjects do lend themselves more to that style of testing. I'll make you a deal," she said, "if I give a test and you think I've graded it unfairly, you may try to convince me of why it was unfair. Maybe it will involve some extra work on your part, because I'm also trying to teach you to communicate clearly what you mean, but I will always give you a hearing. And I'm confident in saying that most of the teachers in this school will be ready to do the same thing. We want our students to succeed, and we would love it if you even enjoyed coming to class." She smiled.

I felt a little dizzy. I'd never dreamed a teacher would say any of that. I could argue about my test answers? I could *pick* my own assignments? "Um, we have a paper coming up," I said. "So, what if I wrote a story about World War I instead of a report?"

She nodded. "I'd want you to include all the same information you would use in a report. In fact, that would be a great challenge for you, making the story interesting and informative at the same time."

I couldn't believe she'd agreed to let me write a story for history class.

"Oh, I have a wonderful idea," she said, her eyes sparkling. "You're good at languages, aren't you?"

"I guess so." I nodded uncertainly.

"If you wanted to translate your story into French or Spanish, I think Mr. O'Dell would let you use it as an assignment, or maybe extra credit."

"I can use a history assignment for a language class?" I asked.

She laughed at my expression. "Take charge of your education," she said. "We want you to learn, and if you prove you are trying we'll help you any way we can."

At lunch that day, I told Priya and Liz what Ms. Atwood had said.

"Oh, yeah," Liz said. "You didn't do that at your last school?"

Priya was shaking her head. "I don't think most schools do that," she said, "but some are better than others. My mother's a teacher; she said it's a lot more work to have the students so involved in making up assignments. It's harder to grade equally when someone writes a report and someone makes a model and someone draws a comic book," she said."

"A comic book?" No wonder Ms. Atwood hadn't seemed shocked at the story idea.

"Steve Westerfeld did a big comic book thing last fall in science about the environmental impact of all kinds of pollution. Mr. Russo loved it."

"Wow," I said, and then, because I was feeling reckless and excited about life for the first time in months, I added, "Hey, did you know that my real name isn't Ann?"

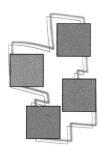

According to gifted expert Kathryn Keirouz, curriculum differentiation includes these typical procedures:

- deleting already mastered material from existing curriculum,
- adding new content, process, or product expectations to existing curriculum,
- extending existing curriculum to provide enrichment activities,
- providing course work for able students at an earlier age than usual, and
- writing new units or courses that meet the needs of gifted students.

Another expert in the field of gifted education, C. J. Maker, suggests that school curriculum needs to be differentiated in terms of:

1. **Learning environment:** The aim is to create a learning environment which encourages students to engage their abilities to the greatest extent possible, including taking risks and building knowledge and skills in what they perceive as a safe, flexible environment. It should be:

   - **student-centered**, focusing on the student's interests, input, and ideas rather than those of the teacher.

   - **encourage independence**, tolerating and encouraging student initiative.

   - **open**, permitting new people, materials, ideas, and things to enter the classroom, and nonacademic and *interdisciplinary* connections to be made.

- **accepting**, encouraging acceptance of others' ideas and opinions before evaluating them.
- **complex**, including a rich variety of resources, media, ideas, methods, and tasks.
- **highly mobile**, encouraging movement in and out of groups, desk settings, classrooms, and schools.

2. **Content modification:** Remove the "ceiling" on what can be learned, and use the student's individual abilities to build a richer and more diverse knowledge base. This can be facilitated by encouraging:

Curriculum differentiation seeks to remove an expected ceiling from each student's achievement, allowing her to reach as high as she can.

- **abstractness**, with content shifting from facts, definitions, and descriptions to concepts, relationships to key concepts, and *generalization*.

- **complexity**, with content shifting to interrelationships rather than considering factors separately.

- **variety**, with content expanding beyond material presented in the normal program.

- **study of people**, including the study of individuals or peoples, and how they have reacted to various opportunities and problems.

- **study of methods of inquiry**, including procedures used by experts working in their fields.

3. **Process modification:** The aim is to promote creativity and higher-level cognitive skills, and to encourage productive use of the knowledge the students have mastered. This can be facilitated by encouraging:

- **higher levels of thinking**, involving cognitive challenges, logical problems, critical thinking, and problem solving.

- **creative thinking**, involving imagination, *intuitive* approaches, and brainstorming techniques.

- **open-endedness**, encouraging risk-taking and stressing there is no single right answer.

- **group interaction**, with motivated students cooperatively encouraging each other's interest in the task.

- **variable pacing**, allowing students to move through lower-order thinking more rapidly as they are able, but allowing more time for students to respond fully on higher-order thinking tasks.

- **a variety of learning processes**, accommodating different students' *learning styles*.

- **debriefing**, encouraging students to put into words their reasoning behind their conclusions to a problem or question.

- **freedom of choice**, involving students in evaluation of choices of topics, methods, products, and environments.

4. **Product modification:** The aim is to facilitate opportunities for all students to produce a learning product that reflects their potential. This can be encouraged by incorporating into the educational program:

- **real problems**, relevant to the student and the activity.

- **real audiences**, which could include another student or group of students, a teacher (not necessarily the class teacher), an assembly, a mentor, a community, or specific interest group.

- **real deadlines**, encouraging time-management skills and realistic planning.

- **transformations**, involving original use of information rather than simple *regurgitation*.

- **appropriate evaluation**, with the learning product and the process of its development being both self-evaluated and evaluated by the product's audience using previously established "real-world" *criteria* that are appropriate for such products.

A number of management strategies are often useful in implementing these curriculum differentiation strategies, including:

- **the use of contracts**, allowing individualized and student-negotiated programs and promoting the development of time-management skills and *autonomy*.

- **conferencing**, allowing student negotiation and review.

- **grouping strategies**, facilitating children to work with each other and encouraging group interaction.

Many educational experts believe that curriculum differentiation is the right answer, not only for meeting the needs of students with special gifts but for meeting the needs of all students. However, the day-to-day, real-life practice of curriculum differentiation requires a major shift in the way many teachers operate—and it may also be demanding to small schools that lack funds for retraining and implementing new programs.

Chapter 7
Learning to Speak New Languages

"Hey, Glory, hand me the glue," Liz said.

I handed her the glue stick and went back to typing. She, Priya, and I were all in my room, working on our English presentation about the women of *The Odyssey*. Liz was arranging pictures of Penelope, Circe, Calypso, and Nausicaa on a poster, while Priya and I put together the PowerPoint presentation. We had also designed a Web site that would have more information than we could give in class.

Ever since I had told them my real name, Priya and Liz have called me Glory. I kind of like it. As long as they don't call me Morning-Glory.

My life was starting to come together. My room looked much better than it did when we'd moved in a month ago. I'd painted two walls dark red, and Priya and Liz had helped me decorate one of them with handwritten quotes, photos, and a few handprints for good measure. I was still deciding what to do with the two remaining white walls. Things had improved at school, too. I liked history and English, and even science class wasn't that bad. Math was still math, but I'd never cared about that anyway.

I kept working on the English presentation after my friends left, even though it wasn't due until the next week. Mostly, I was playing with the Web site. I kept finding more and more information online that I wanted to put in. And I took a long time trying to decide which colors and fonts looked best on the main page. I was very picky; I wanted the Web site to look professional.

I woke up the next morning at six o'clock with my head on my desk. My neck was sore, and when I looked at myself in the mirror, I saw that the keyboard had left indentations on my face. I had no idea what time I'd fallen asleep.

By the time I got to school, I was mostly awake, and fortunately, the keyboard print on my cheek had faded. Then I walked into math class and discovered we had a test. A test? Could it be a pop quiz? Frantically, I looked through the syllabus and discovered that, no, it was a scheduled test that I was supposed to know about.

Ms. Vinizi put the test on my desk and I looked at it blankly, trying to remember what we'd been talking about last class. I had no problem adding and subtracting, multiplying and dividing, but math was never that simple anymore. The equations were full of *x*s and *y*s, fractions and parentheses. I was too tired to remember what I was supposed to do with them all. I did my best, but I just wanted to go to sleep.

The next day, Ms. Atwood called me up to her desk again during homeroom.

"You had a math test yesterday," she said. "How do you think you did on it?"

"Not very well," I said.

"What happened?" she asked.

"I forgot there was a test," I said. "But I'm not any good at math anyway."

"Maybe," she said. "Nobody's good at everything. But I don't want you not to try because you already think you can't do it."

I sighed. "Math is so boring. It's not like I'm going to be a math teacher or anything."

"What if you wanted to be a doctor?"

"I don't, but doctors don't use math anyway, do they?"

"Sure they do," she said. "To be a doctor you need to take chemistry, and there's lots of math in chemistry. In fact, you'll find that math is one of those things that keep popping up in unexpected places. Really," she went on, "every job will have some parts that are interesting and some that are boring. It's good for you to learn how to do boring things sometimes; sneak them in around the interesting stuff like crushing up bad-tasting medicine in a spoonful of choco-late sauce."

"I don't think there *are* any interesting parts in math," I said.

"I think you'd be surprised. Why don't you talk to Ms. Vinizi about it?"

I really didn't want to talk to Ms. Vinizi. Especially after she handed back the test and I discovered I had failed. I thought, though, that Ms. Atwood would probably ask me what Ms. Vinizi had said, and, even if she didn't, she'd prob-ably be talking to her about it in the staff room. Somehow, I didn't want to disappoint Ms. Atwood.

"Could I talk to you for a minute?" I asked Ms. Vinizi after class. "Ms. Atwood said I should ask you what's inter-esting about math."

She laughed. "Why do you think math *isn't* interest-ing?"

"It's all those numbers and letters and nothing means anything."

"What?" She looked astonished. "Why do you think they don't mean anything?"

"Adding and subtracting were common sense," I said. "But now we just make complicated equations and move things around."

"Don't you know," she asked, "that math is the language of the world? People can take these equations and use them to figure out how our universe works. When you learn a new language," she went on, "you need to learn the grammar and the vocabulary in order to understand and use the language. It's the same way in math. What we are learning now is equivalent to the grammar of the universe."

I'd never thought of math as a language. It had always seemed to be disconnected from reality, no matter how many word problems teachers contrived. I imagined the world speaking the language of math and, for the first time, I wanted to understand.

After that, my math grades improved. I still make stupid mistakes, and it isn't my best subject, but I actually want to try to understand. I discovered, too, that I like pushing the equation one way and another until all the complicated looking parts fall away and the simplicity of the solution is the only thing left.

So, somehow, after all my work to be normal and fit in, I became a "smart kid." Mostly, that just meant I did well in school, so it was okay. Only a few people called me "brain," but since the teachers all tried to get everyone to do well, it wasn't that big a deal. And I had Priya and Liz, which helped a lot.

Then summer came. My parents were so overjoyed that I was actually being the good little girl and getting good grades, that they signed me up for summer classes. They kept saying how great it was that we'd moved to Maddox where there were so many opportunities. Daniel was going too, although he was also going to sports camp, so he only had to take one physics class. Since he's the perfect child, he loved it. Mom and Dad had let me help decide which classes I would take, but I didn't want to take any.

"Pick four," Dad had said, beaming, as he plunked the shiny brochure down in front of me. The classes were offered by a local university and were intended for kids just like me—supposedly brilliant students who just couldn't bear to be away from school for a whole summer. I thought I was doing pretty well to finally think school was okay at all, and I could really use a break. Priya's family had invited me to go to the beach with them for two weeks, for one thing, and I wouldn't be able to go if I was taking classes. That argument didn't work with Dad and Mom, though.

"Just think of how great it will be," Mom said enthusiastically. "You'll be meeting other smart kids and getting to think and learn!"

"Priya and Liz are smart," I said. "And I think and learn all the time. Just this morning I learned that if you throw a pen out the window it doesn't usually stick point-first in the lawn."

"Why were you throwing pens out the window?" Daniel asked from the other side of the kitchen table.

I shrugged. "They were out of ink."

"That's not the kind of thing I meant," Mom said.

"You'd better go out and pick up those pens before I mow the lawn this afternoon," Dad said.

Since they refused to budge on the summer school thing, I finally picked out a novel-writing class that didn't look bad.

"Great," Dad said. "Now pick three more."

After a great deal of argument, we decided on astronomy, Hitchcock films, and introductory Japanese as the other three courses.

When I got into them, the classes were all pretty interesting. There were about ten or twelve kids in each class, and we usually sat around in a circle and talked. The film class was especially good that way, but every course had its perks. For astronomy, we got to lie around on a hill in the middle of the night, pointing out stars and constellations. We took field trips in Japanese class, like going to a Japanese restaurant and trying to order lunch or visiting the Asian art gallery downtown. We critiqued each other's novels and raced each other to see who could write the most words over a weekend.

Even though I hadn't wanted to take the summer classes, I was having fun at first. Then, sometime toward the end of July, I realized I was getting stressed out. I always had homework, even if it was only to watch a movie. I hardly ever got to see Priya and Liz anymore because I was too busy writing my novel or practicing Japanese or whatever. The kids in the summer program were all really smart, and I felt like I had to push myself to keep up sometimes. I found myself daydreaming about hanging out with Priya at the beach—looking at cute guys and reading trashy romances—but then I pushed those thoughts away because I didn't have time for them.

I also started drinking coffee in July. I felt like I didn't sleep much anymore. If I wasn't out on an astronomy field trip, I was up making sure my novel didn't sound stupid, or deciding what insightful comments to make about *Rear Window*. I didn't want to look dumb in front of the other students.

I was working on my novel one evening when the computer dinged to tell me I had new e-mail. I was just on the verge of figuring out what my main character would say to her unhappy mother to explain just how messed up their relationship was and how she wanted things to be better between them, so I was annoyed that the ding had interrupted my train of thought.

The e-mail was from Priya.

Hey Glory, I just got back from the beach this afternoon. It was great; I wish you could have come. I haven't seen you in forever!! We really need to get together and hang out. I think Liz's family should be back from her grandmother's house tomorrow. We should have a sleepover or something. You know, watch stupid movies, eat popcorn, dye our hair with Kool-Aid . . . Let me know. See ya, Priya.

It all sounded so normal that, inexplicably, I burst into tears. Suddenly, no matter how much I liked my summer classes, I didn't want to do it anymore.

I cried for an hour. I couldn't think of what to do. Mom and Dad would never let me drop out. I wondered if I should run away from home. Then I thought of Ms. Atwood.

I found Ms. Atwood's address and phone number online, but I was too nervous to call her. What would I say? I hated talking on the phone to anyone but my best friends. I figured out where she lived—the online map said it was 3.1 miles from my house—and thought maybe I could walk over there and talk to her in person.

After I'd started walking, I felt stupid. What if she wasn't home? What if she didn't want to talk to me? I kept walking, though. I looked at the kids playing along the streets in the warm summer evening, and I tried not to think about anything at all.

I got to her house at nearly eight o'clock. A dusty blue minivan was in the driveway, so I thought maybe she was home. Now that I was there, I didn't know if I had the courage to ring the doorbell.

Just then, a little boy came running around the corner of the house. He was followed by a little girl of about the same age and then by a man. They all stopped and looked at me as I hesitated on their front walk.

"Can I help you?" the man asked.

"Um, Mr. Atwood?" I asked.

"Yes."

"Ah, I was in your wife's class last year," I began, and then stopped. I felt like a complete idiot. Not to mention a stalker.

"Oh, hold on a second." He opened the front door of the house and leaned inside. I couldn't hear what he said, but then Ms. Atwood appeared in the doorway.

"Ann! How are you? Come in." She didn't even ask why I was there.

Ten minutes later, sitting in Ms. Atwood's living room, I found myself pouring out the whole story of summer school and not getting to go to the beach with Priya, and how I really liked the summer classes but they were getting to be too much. She looked thoughtful.

"Have you talked to your parents about this?"

"I can't. They didn't listen in the beginning when I said I didn't want to do it. They're never going to let me drop out now."

"What if I talk to them with you?"

So she drove me home. Mom and Dad hadn't noticed I was gone, since I spent so much time working in my room these days, and they were surprised to see me walk into the house with Ms. Atwood.

Mom and Dad took it better than I'd feared. Maybe it was because Ms. Atwood was sitting right there so they couldn't yell at me.

"This just isn't fun anymore," I finished. "I just want to be able to hang out with my friends and enjoy the summer."

"We want that, too," Mom said, "but we wanted you to have all the opportunities you didn't have in Mill Creek, all the things we didn't get to do when we were younger that now we wish we could have done."

"I don't want you to develop an attitude of quitting when something is hard," Dad said.

My first instinct was to jump in and yell that I didn't care if I turned into a quitter; I just wanted to be happy.

I took a deep breath. "I think," I said slowly, "that maybe I need to learn how to step back when I'm overloaded and not try to do too much at the same time."

Mom and Dad were nodding thoughtfully, which I thought was a good sign.

"What if you didn't drop them all?" Dad suggested. "Maybe just the one that's giving you the most trouble."

"None of them are giving me trouble, but all of them are taking a lot of time." I thought for a moment. "What if I dropped two?"

In the end, Mom and Dad agreed to let me drop astronomy and Japanese. I liked both the classes, and I was a bit sad about not going back, but I was a lot more relieved than sad. I kept the novel-writing class and the film class because they seemed the least like work. Priya and Liz started watching the movies with me, and that improved the summer a lot, too.

When school started again, I was almost excited about it. I'm starting to be okay with being who I am. I think Ms. Atwood helped me see what learning really could be. The future stretching out in front of me seems hopeful now instead of bleak. I'm still working on my novel, too.

I used to feel like everyone at school was speaking a language they all understood but I didn't. I knew there were other people like me, because I'd met them online, but I'd never met them in person. I imagined that I'd spend the rest of my life being this weird brainy geek who didn't fit in anywhere but cyberspace. The stories I wrote were just for me, because I figured no one else would understand or like them.

But maybe when my novel is finished, I'll try to get it published.

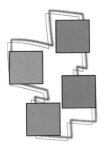

Studies show that when kids with special gifts don't receive some kind of adapted educational program, they are less likely to excel. For instance, children with special gifts who spend 25 to 50 percent of class time merely waiting for other students may engage in self-stimulating behavior, such as counting their teeth with their tongue, daydreaming, drawing, tapping a foot, or entertaining themselves by distracting other students. These actions interfere not only with their own learning, but they can also render the entire classroom less effective for all students. Boredom can have other consequences as well. If students who are gifted and talented never meet a challenge in school, they may not develop the coping skills necessary to persevere through challenges later in life, noted Paula Olszewski-Kubilius, director of the Center for Talent Development at Northwestern University.

Ways That Gifted Kids Cope

Here's how some kids with special talents cope.

1. Pretend not to know as much as they really do.

2. Act like a brain so people will leave them alone.

3. Disguise their abilities.

4. Avoid gifted/talented programs altogether.

5. Use their talents in places other than school (such as community or church events).

6. Spend more time with adults.

7. Be friends only with other young people who are as gifted/talented as they are.

8. Develop the humility to accept and share their talents to help their peers.

Which of these coping mechanisms do you think are the most productive?

Our society tends to be unkind to those who don't fit in. This is particularly true for adolescents. Kids who are different in some way (whether because they have unusual intelligence, a physical challenge, or a mental disability) are often teased or **ostracized**. This makes the teen years very difficult for those kids who face the challenge of being different.

But ultimately, what matters most in life isn't whether you're intelligent or not so intelligent, whether you have amazing talents or the more average, everyday kind. Each individual in the world is valuable, and each has something special to offer those around her. What matters most is this: Are we using whatever talents we've been given to make the world a better place? Do we use our talents for kindness—or are we selfish, seeking only to get more for ourselves?

Think about it: Who is worth more to the world—a person with a high IQ who is cruel and self-serving, or a person with low cognitive skills who is always kind and sensitive to other's feelings, always seeking to share his skills? Which gifts are the most necessary to our world—intelligence or kindness, academic achievement or generosity? What would the world be like if we all shared our gifts with others?

What do you think?

Glossary

ambiguity: A situation in which something can be understood in more than one way, and it is unclear which meaning is intended.

asynchronous: Not happening at the same time.

autonomy: Independence and the capacity to make moral decisions and act on them.

criteria: Accepted standards used in making decisions or judgments about something.

criterion: The singular form of criteria.

extroverted: Having the characteristics of being sociable, self-confident, and outgoing with other people.

finesse: Elegant ability.

generalization: The process by which a learned response is made to a stimulus similar to but not identical to the original stimulus.

initiative: The ability to act and make decisions without the help or advice of other people.

interdisciplinary: Involving two or more academic, scientific, or artistic fields of study.

intuition: The state of being aware or of knowing something without having to discover or perceive it.

intuitive: Known or perceived by intuition rather than rational thought or the senses.

kinesthetic: Having to do with the sensory experiences that come from body movements.

learning styles: Preferred ways by which people learn.

longitudinal: Involving the repeated examination of a set of test subjects over time with respect to one or more study variable.

ostracized: Banished or excluded.

precocious: More developed, especially mentally, than is usual or expected at a particular developmental stage.

psychomotor: Relating to actions that proceed from mental activity.

regurgitation: The act of repeating or reproducing what has been read, heard, or taught in away that shows no personal thought or understanding.

retains: Is able to recall ideas or information.

spatial: Relating to, occupying, or happening in space.

standardized: Removed variations and irregularities and made all types or examples of something the same or brought them into conformity with one another.

subtleties: Distinctions that are difficult to make but are important.

Western: Found in or typical of countries, especially in Europe and North and South America, whose culture and society are greatly influenced by traditions rooted in Greek and Roman culture and in Christianity.

Further Reading

Clark, B. *Growing Up Gifted: Developing the Potential of Children at Home and at School.* Upper Saddle River, N.J.: Prentice-Hall, 2002.

Davidson, Jan, and Bob Davidson. *Genius Denied: How to Stop Wasting Our Brightest Young Minds.* New York: Simon & Schuster, 2004.

Delisle, James R., and Judy Galbraith. *When Gifted Kids Don't Have All the Answers: How to Meet Their Social and Emotional Needs.* New York: Free Spirit, 2002.

Galbraith, Judy, and James R. Delisle. *The Gifted Kids' Survival Guide: A Teen Handbook.* New York: Free Spirit, 2000.

Neihart, Maureen. *The Social and Emotional Development of Gifted Children: What Do We Know?* Waco, Tex.: Prufrock Press, 2001.

For More Information

American Association for Gifted Children
www.aagc.org

American Psychological Association Center for Gifted
Education
www.apa.org/ed/cgep.html

Gifted Child Society
www.gifted.org

Hoagies Gifted Education
www.hoagiesgifted.org/parents.htm

National Association for Gifted Children
www.nagc.org

National Foundation for Gifted and Creative Children
www.nfgcc.org

Publisher's note:
The Web sites listed on this page were active at the time of publication. The publisher
is not responsible for Web sites that have changed their addresses or discontinued
operation since the date of publication. The publisher will review and update the
Web-site list upon each reprint.

Bibliography

Bee, H. *Child and Adolescent Development*. Boston, Mass.: Pearson Custom Publishing, 2004.

Buescher, Thomas M., and Sharon Higham. *Helping Adolescents Adjust to Giftedness*. ERIC EC Digest #E489, ERIC Clearinghouse on Disabilities and Gifted Education, Reston, Virginia, 2006.

Dauber, S., and C. Benbow. "National Association for Gifted Children." *Gifted Child Quarterly* 34(1990): 10–14.

ERIC EC Digest #E476, ERIC Clearinghouse on Handicapped and Gifted Children, Reston, Virginia, 2006.

Farmer, David. "Curriculum Differentiation." http://www. austega.com/gifted/provisions/curdifferent.htm.

Fasko, D., Jr. "An Analysis of Multiple Intelligences Theory and Its Use with the Gifted and Talented. *Roeper Review* 23(2003): 126–130.

Feldmen, R. *Essentials of Understanding Psychology* (4th ed.). Amherst: University of Massachusetts, 2000.

Jacobsen, M. "Tips for Parents: The Real World of Gifted Teens." Davidson Institute for Talent Development, 2003. http://www.gt-cybersource.org/Record.aspx?NavID=2_0&rid=12366.

Kaplan, Leslie S. "Helping Gifted Students with Stress Management." ERIC EC Digest #E488, ERIC Clearinghouse on Handicapped and Gifted Children, Reston, Virginia, 2006.

Karnes, F. and S. Bean (eds.). *Methods and Materials for Teaching the Gifted*. Waco, Tex.: Prufrock Press, 2000.

Lidz, C. S., and S. L. Macrine. "An Alternative Approach to the Identification of Gifted Culturally and Linguistically Diverse Learners: The Contribution of Dynamic Assessment." *School Psychology International* 22(2001): 74–96.

Index

Picture Credits

iStock: pp. 40, 100
        Ahvo, Jahnne: p. 39
        Argyropoulos, George: p. 20
        Carroll, Jamie: p. 90
        Felton, Julie: p. 28
        Hudson, Christopher: p. 61
        Kim Goh, Li: p. 17
        Monu, Nicholas: p. 86
        Serrabossa, Eva: p. 18
        Stay, Mark: pp. 42, 85, 88
        Tero, Dan: p. 72
Karim, Jawed: p. 24

To the best knowledge of the publisher, all other images are in the public domain. If any image has been inadvertently uncredited, please notify Harding House Publishing Service, Vestal, New York 13850, so that rectification can be made for future printings.

Authors

Sheila Nelson is a freelance writer, the author of nearly two dozen educational books for children and young adults. She lives in Rochester, New York, with her husband and two children.

Phyllis Livingston has degrees in both psychology and special education. She has worked with many young adults who had special gifts.

Series Consultants

Dr. Bridgemohan is an Assistant Professor in Pediatrics at Harvard Medical School and is a Board Certified Developmental-Behavioral Pediatrician on staff in the Developmental Medicine Center at Children's Hospital, Boston. She specializes in assessment and treatment of autism and developmental disorders in young children. Her clinical practice includes children and youth with autism, developmental language disorders, global delays, mental retardation, attentional and learning disorders, anxiety, and depression. Dr. Bridgemohan is Co-director of residency training in Child Development at Children's Hospital, Boston, and is co-editor of "Bright Futures Case Studies for Primary Care Clinicians: Child Development and Behavior," a curriculum used nationwide in Pediatric Residency training programs. Dr. Bridgemohan has also published research and review articles on resident education, toilet training, autism screening, and medical evaluation of children with developmental disorders.

Cindy Croft, M.A.Ed., is the Director of the Center for Inclusive Child Care (CICC) at Concordia University, St. Paul, MN. The CICC is a comprehensive resource network for promoting and supporting inclusive early childhood and school-age programs and providers with Project EXCEPTIONAL training and consultation, and other resources at www.inclusivechildcare. org. In addition to working with the CICC, Ms. Croft is on the faculty at Concordia University and Minneapolis Community and Technical College.

DATE DUE